CHINESE
GODS, HEROES, AND MYTHOLOGY

BY TAMMY GAGNE

CONTENT CONSULTANT
Zhihui Sophia Geng
Associate Professor of Chinese
College of Saint Benedict and Saint John's University

Cover image: Dragons appear in many Chinese myths and legends.

Core Library

An Imprint of Abdo Publishing
abdobooks.com

abdocorelibrary.com

Published by Abdo Publishing, a division of ABDO, PO Box 398166, Minneapolis, Minnesota 55439. Copyright © 2019 by Abdo Consulting Group, Inc. International copyrights reserved in all countries. No part of this book may be reproduced in any form without written permission from the publisher. Core Library™ is a trademark and logo of Abdo Publishing.

Printed in the United States of America, North Mankato, Minnesota
092018
012019

THIS BOOK CONTAINS
RECYCLED MATERIALS

Cover Photo: iStockphoto
Interior Photos: iStockphoto, 1; Hung Chung Chih/Shutterstock Images, 4–5; Shutterstock Images, 7, 9, 10, 34–35, 39, 43, 45; Chen Yuefeng/Imaginechina/AP Images, 14–15; Ignacio Salaverria/Shutterstock Images, 17; WhyMePhoto/Shutterstock Images, 20–21; DeAgostini/Getty Images, 24–25; The Picture Art Collection/Alamy Stock Photo, 26–27; Pictures From History/Newscom, 29, 30; Huang He Ly/Imaginechina/AP Images, 32; Elisaveta Ivanova/iStockphoto, 37; Vincent Yu/AP Images, 40

Editor: Marie Pearson
Series Designer: Ryan Gale

Library of Congress Control Number: 2018949762

Publisher's Cataloging-in-Publication Data

Names: Gagne, Tammy, author.
Title: Chinese gods, heroes, and mythology / by Tammy Gagne.
Description: Minneapolis, Minnesota : Abdo Publishing, 2019 | Series: Gods, heroes, and mythology | Includes online resources and index.
Identifiers: ISBN 9781532117800 (lib. bdg.) | ISBN 9781532170669 (ebook)
Subjects: LCSH: Chinese mythology--Juvenile literature. | Chinese gods--Juvenile literature. | Heroes--Juvenile literature.
Classification: DDC 299.51--dc23

CONTENTS

THE WEAVER AND THE COWHERD

One of the most popular stories in Chinese culture is that of Niulang and Zhinu. Niulang had a modest life. He lived in a small cottage and made his living as a cowherd. His only friend was an old ox that he kept on his property.

One day Niulang discovered that his ox could talk. The animal explained that he had once been a star in the night sky. He told his human friend that he should preserve his hide after his death. He said this magical item could carry a mere mortal all the way to the heavens.

Oxen, important animals for farming, have long been a part of traditional stories in many cultures.

The ox also encouraged Niulang to visit a nearby pond. A beautiful weaver named Zhinu often visited it to bathe. When Niulang arrived, she was there. As soon as the pair met, they fell in love. When Niulang asked Zhinu to marry him, she agreed.

Shortly after their marriage, Zhinu gave birth to twins, a boy and a girl. They named the twins Brother Gold and Sister Jade. As time went on, the beloved ox died. The couple lived on happily together in the small cottage with their children. But Zhinu was no ordinary woman. She was the granddaughter of the Jade Emperor, an important god, and she was a goddess in her own right. She was in charge of weaving clouds for the sky. When the Emperor

FOLK SONGS

Not all myths are told in prose, or story form. Many Chinese myths are told through poems and songs. People sing these songs at events such as weddings and funerals. Often the songs consist of several myths combined.

Figures of the Jade Emperor can still be seen in shrines today.

found out about the marriage, everything changed. He was angry that Zhinu had married a mortal. He sent his wife to retrieve their granddaughter.

Niulang came home one day to find his children all alone. They told him that a woman had kidnapped their mother. Suddenly, Niulang realized who his wife really was. Luckily, he had done as the ox instructed upon his death. Niulang grabbed the magical hide and headed for the heavens with his children.

When the Empress saw them, she created a large river in the heavens. She wanted to use it to keep the couple apart for eternity. But then the Empress saw Niulang and his children crying. She felt sad for them. She told them that they could meet with Zhinu one day each year. On this day, she said, magpies would form a magical bridge over the rough waters. She then turned them all into stars, and the river became the Milky Way.

People now celebrate this magical day, called Qixi in China, similar to the way people in the West celebrate

STORIES IN THE
STARS

According to Chinese mythology, the star called Altair was once the cowherd Niulang. Zhinu became Vega. Between Altair and Vega is the Milky Way. Altair and Vega are also two of the stars included in the Western constellation known as the Summer Triangle. The third star of this triangle is called Deneb. How does the Milky Way resemble the river that separates Zhinu from her husband and children?

VEGA
(ZHINU)

DENEB

MILKY WAY

ALTAIR
(NIULANG)

Valentine's Day. Some people think it is special when it rains on this day. They say the rain comes from Zhinu crying tears of joy when she sees her husband and children again.

MANY PEOPLE, MANY STORIES

Chinese mythology is made up of myths that often involve gods, goddesses, and the supernatural. They are not always based on facts. Yet they tell truths that more realistic-sounding stories cannot. Chinese myths come from the country's 56 different ethnic groups. These groups include the Han people, who make up most of China's population. The story of Zhinu and Niulang is part of Han mythology. Some of China's stories were recorded in ancient writings that date back 3,000 years. Other stories were passed down orally. Some were even told through paintings on shells or bones.

Like the mythology of other cultures, these stories include powerful gods and goddesses and a variety of

China is a large country with a rich history and a diverse tradition of myths and stories.

RESPECTED RESOURCES

Many experts consider *Shanhaijing* to be the most important book about Chinese mythology. It was written as late as the 100s BCE. This book includes parts of many myths. It also offers details about ancient geography, history, and medicine. No one knows for sure who wrote this book. Most people think it has many different authors. Another highly respected text is *Sou shen ji*. This one was written by Gan Bao, who lived in the 300s CE.

magical creatures. The religions Buddhism, Confucianism, and Taoism all feature some of these stories. Some myths explain how the world was created. Others teach lessons about how people should treat one another. Many religious followers do not take these stories literally. But the myths reflect the values that people use to guide their lives.

STRAIGHT TO THE
SOURCE

Lihui Yang and Deming An wrote the *Handbook of Chinese Mythology*. In this book, they explain how Chinese myths became a source for the arts in China:

> Chinese myths have long been thought to be the root of Chinese literature and art. Myths have had a great impact on writers. During the history of Chinese literature, many eminent poets and writers . . . were all more or less nourished by Chinese myths. Some of them directly took myths as their writing material, and some further absorbed from myths stylistic techniques such as exaggeration, fantasy, and fiction. By doing this, these literary figures developed a strong romantic writing style in Chinese literature, which is thought to originate from myths.

> Source: Lihui Yang and Deming An. *Handbook of Chinese Mythology*. Santa Barbara, CA: ABC-CLIO, 2005. Print. 50.

Back It Up

The authors of this passage use evidence to support a point. Write a paragraph describing the point the authors are making. Then write down two or three pieces of evidence the authors use to make the point.

轩 辕 黄 帝

CHINESE GODS AND GODDESSES

Chinese mythology teaches that all Chinese people descend from Huang Di, the Yellow Emperor. Many stories tell about Huang Di, who is also known as the Thunder God. One of them links his birth in approximately 2704 BCE to the stars. One night, Huang Di's mother, Fubao, noticed something odd in the night sky. She saw a bolt of lightning that completely surrounded a star. In Chinese myths, events related to the stars and planets are said to foretell important births and deaths. Soon, Fubao realized she was pregnant. After Huang Di was born, he quickly

A huge statue of the Yellow Emperor sits in Xinzheng, China.

proved to be a remarkable child. He could speak when he was just a baby. He was especially wise throughout his 300 years of life.

THE INVENTOR OF CHINESE WRITING

Western writing systems use letters for sounds. Chinese writing is made up of many symbols that may stand for sounds or entire words. Cangjie was the mythical creator of Chinese writing. He worked for Huang Di. Cangjie was said to have four eyes. He spent a great deal of time looking at the world around him. He studied things like bird feathers and turtle shells. All of these objects became his inspiration for the Chinese written language. The Chinese gods were so happy with the creation of writing that they made grain rain down from the sky.

XIHE AND CHANGXI

Many Chinese myths explain how the stars and planets came into being. In one Buddhist story, Xihe, a wife of a god named Emperor Jun, gives birth to ten suns. Only one sun appears in the sky at any time. Xihe spends her time getting the others ready for their turns. After each sun travels across the sky, he returns to Xihe

As the brightest object in the night sky, the moon became a natural reference point for many stories and myths.

covered in dust. She bathes him in the Gang Gulf so he can shine again.

A similar myth tells the story of Changxi, another wife of Emperor Jun. Changxi is the mother of the ten moons. The moons take turns in the night sky just as the suns do. After each one finishes his job, Changxi washes him at Mount Riyue. Then he gets in line for his next turn to shine in the night sky.

XIWANGMU

The Chinese goddess of immortality is Xiwangmu. She is known for serving her guests divine peaches that make people immortal. Xiwangmu has a fierce appearance and nature. Although she mostly looks like a human, she has the teeth of a tiger and a panther's tail. She also roars.

Xiwangmu is the leader of many other goddesses. Myths about Xiwangmu show her as controlling many parts of people's lives. In these stories she rules over health and wealth, as well as disease and punishment.

SHENTU AND YULÜ

Known as the Gate Gods, Shentu and Yulü have an important job. A giant peach tree grows atop Dushuo Mountain. The branches extend far into the air, high enough to reach the gate where ghosts travel between the worlds. Shentu and Yulü stand watch at this gate. When an evil ghost tries to pass through, they tie it up in reeds and feed it to tigers. Huang Di encouraged people to paint pictures of these gods on the doors to their homes. Doing this, along with placing a statue made from peach tree wood and some reed rope outside, kept evil spirits away.

STRAIGHT TO THE
SOURCE

Jaling Chen is the principal dancer with Shen Yun Performing Arts. This group's dances are inspired by Chinese history and culture. In an interview, Chen shared her thoughts about the role of spiritual tradition in both her performances and Chinese culture:

> China was once known as 'The Celestial Empire' and 'The Land of the Divine.' And Chinese mythology is filled with accounts of semi-divine beings coexisting with humans on Earth. . . .
>
> These deities are said to have left a rich culture of music, dance, and other arts. In fact, you could say we attribute all aspects of traditional Chinese culture to divine intervention. This includes Chinese language, attire, medicine, architecture. . . . Ancient Chinese believed they were living in a land guided by the divine. They were living a lifestyle created by the divine.
>
> Source: Jaling Chen. "Dancing Ancient Culture." *Shen Yun Performing Arts*. Shen Yun, 2018. Web. Accessed June 29, 2018.

What's the Big Idea?

Take a closer look at Chen's words. What is her main idea? What evidence is used to support this point? Write a few sentences explaining how Chen uses evidence to support her main point.

CREATURES OF CHINESE MYTHOLOGY

Chinese mythology is filled with many wondrous creatures. One of them is Yinglong. This winged dragon helped Huang Di in a great battle against Chiyou. Chiyou was the god of war. So Huang Di and Yinglong needed to be clever to defeat him. The dragon gathered great amounts of water to cause massive floods. The emperor also asked for the help of Ba, the drought goddess. She made sure that a long period without rain followed the flooding. In this myth, Huang Di kills his enemy using a drought.

Dragons play important roles in Chinese mythology.

THE ANIMAL OF TRUTH

In Chinese mythology, Xiezhi is a goat with black fur, hooves, and a horn. This animal is also known as the animal of truth. When honesty comes into question, Xiezhi is said to point its horn at whoever is lying or in the wrong. In some myths, the goat also kills the guilty party.

Because Yinglong had the ability to gather water, many Chinese people see the creature as controlling the rain. After its work with Huang Di was done, Yinglong moved to the south. According to one story, this is why that region gets so much rain. Chinese people in other areas often ask for Yinglong's help during droughts. They build a clay statue of the dragon, hoping that rain will soon fall from the sky.

XIANGLIU

Another creature from Chinese mythology is Xiangliu. This giant black snake has nine human heads. It is said that this monster turned all land it traveled over into large gullies where no animals could survive. It was eventually killed by the Chinese hero Yu. But even in death this monster created problems for the Chinese people. When the snake died, its blood poisoned the earth nearby. Crops could not be planted there.

A Taoist myth about Xiangliu describes it as a slightly different kind of creature. This story states that Xiangliu is a nine-headed dragon that eats humans and livestock. It causes floods and other disasters wherever it goes. In this myth, Xiangliu is killed by Nüwa, the goddess who is said to have created people.

SUANNI

Suanni is a lion that is the offspring of dragons. Stories about the creature describe it as fierce enough to eat tigers when it is angered. But it is also known for its patience and calm nature.

KUI

Of all the creatures in Chinese mythology, Kui might well be the strangest. This water monster is described

Mythological creatures of all kinds can be found in ancient Chinese art and decorations.

as looking like an ox but with no horns and only one leg. Kui lived on the mythical Mount Liubo in the East Sea. Whenever Kui dove into the water, a terrible storm would follow. Kui was said to be as bright as the sun and as loud as thunder. After catching this creature, Huang Di used its hide to make a drum. The instrument could be heard from hundreds of miles away.

The philosopher Confucius told a different version of the tale about Kui. Confucius described Kui as a human musician and government official instead of a one-legged monster. He applied the Chinese term *yi zu* to Kui. *Yi zu* has a double meaning. One definition is "one leg." The other is "one is enough." Confucius used the double meaning to make the point that any ruler needs only one good official—one is enough.

STORIES OF CREATION AND DESTRUCTION

According to Chinese mythology, the world was created from the body of the first divine human being, Pangu. As he died, his body started changing into the various parts of the universe. His breath became the wind and clouds. His blood became the rivers. His left eye became the sun while his right one became the moon.

This Taoist creation story is told by many different Chinese ethnic groups. It is popular with the Han people as well as the Miao, Yao,

A portrait of Pangu was created for a Chinese encyclopedia in the early 1600s.

Zhuang, and many other groups. The details are a bit different with each group. But all the stories have two things in common. All the myths state that Pangu himself was born from an egg. They also all support the idea that his dying body transformed into the universe.

HEAVEN AND EARTH

Many Chinese myths tell the story of how heaven and Earth became two different places. In the beginning there was only a small space between them. According to one popular story, the god of war Chiyou was behind the split. A terrible influence on humans, he taught them to lie, cheat, and steal. The leader of the gods ordered the gods Zhong and Li to separate heaven and earth. This made it impossible for the gods to descend to Earth ever again.

NÜWA

The Han credit the goddess Nüwa with creating humans. They say she molded them from mud. She took pieces of the earth into her hands and sculpted these first men and women. The process took Nüwa a great deal

Nüwa is sometimes shown as being part snake.

of time. The work exhausted her. Toward the end, she dragged a cord through the mud before lifting it and shaking it. The pieces of mud that fell off it also became human beings.

As some people tell the story, the humans that Nüwa carefully molded with her hands became the higher classes of human society. They included the rich and noble. The humans that formed from the splattered mud from the cord became people of lower rank.

THE MYTHOLOGY OF CHINESE MEDICINE

Shennong is the god of Chinese medicine. Stories about him explain how he discovered that herbs could heal sicknesses. Shennong tasted hundreds of different plants to see what each one did. He learned how some could heal illnesses. Others were poisonous. But because he was a god, they did not kill him.

Nüwa is often depicted alongside her brother, Fu Xi.

Flooding on the Yellow River still affects China today.

THE GREAT FLOOD

The Yellow River in China often floods, causing
destruction. Because of this, floods appear in many
Chinese myths. The story of Gun and Yu tells how a
father and son devoted their lives to stopping a flood.
Gun, the father, tried to accomplish this task by stealing
soil from Huang Di. He planned to use the soil to absorb
all the water. At first this seemed like a brilliant strategy.
But tragically, Gun was killed while trying to carry out
his plan.

As Gun died, a son named Yu was born from his belly. Yu took over his father's mission to end the flood and save his people. The moral of this story is the importance of never giving up on an important task. Yu continued to work at his goal until he succeeded by digging an enormous channel for all the water. Although it took him 13 years, he never quit. He focused on his goal until he met it. Yu is seen as a hero in Chinese mythology.

EXPLORE ONLINE

The focus of Chapter Four is on the stories of Chinese mythology. The article below focuses on stories of Chinese floods. As you know, every source is different. How is the information on this website different from the information in this chapter? What details are the same? How do the two sources present facts differently?

GEOLOGICAL EVIDENCE MAY SUPPORT CHINESE FLOOD LEGEND

abdocorelibrary.com/chinese-mythology

CHINESE MYTHOLOGY TODAY

Today, the majority of people in China do not practice an organized religion. The nation's communist government officially believes in no gods. But many in China continue to follow religions. The most common religion is Buddhism. About 18 percent of people are Buddhist.

A smaller part of the population practices Taoism. About 1 percent are Taoist.

The lines between different religions sometimes blur. For example, many Buddhists take part in Taoist rituals. Some practices, like Confucianism, are seen as a way of life instead

Modern tourists can visit the Temple of Heaven in Beijing, China.

GUARDIAN LIONS

One example of Chinese mythology's legacy today is the practice of putting guardian lions on houses. These statues are believed to protect the building and the people within. There are usually two lions, one female and one male. The male lion holds a ball representing the world. The female lion is shown protecting a cub.

of a religion. Even for those who are not religious, mythology lives on in many parts of Chinese culture.

VISITING TEMPLES

Chinese people still honor the gods from various myths by visiting the temples of these deities. Different types of temples in China share many symbols and styles. Most temples are open from sunrise to sunset each day. People can easily visit whenever they want.

A common practice among visitors to temples is burning incense. Many temples sell these fragrant items

Lighting sticks of incense is common at temples in China.

outside the structures. Visitors usually light the incense and hold onto it while they pray. Spending time at a temple is considered a highly private practice. People should never take a photograph without the permission of someone who works at the temple.

RESPECT FOR LOYAL COMPANIONS

Chinese myths are not just something people look to on holidays and other important occasions. Myths have also affected the way many Chinese people live their everyday lives. The Yao people tell of the dog Panhu. He is said to be one of their ancestors. In one story, Panhu saves the life of his owner, Emperor Ku. Because of these stories, the Yao people make sure they always treat dogs with respect.

CHINESE NEW YEAR

The Chinese New Year is linked to mythology. On the Chinese calendar, 12 animals take turns representing each year. The Jade Emperor chose these animals by holding a great river race. Every animal in China took part in the event.

THE CHINESE ZODIAC

In Chinese astrology, the zodiac is said to affect people's personalities. For example, people born in the Year of the Dog are believed to be trustworthy. The Year of the Monkey is linked to being charismatic. Those who come into the world in the Year of the Dragon are said to be charming. Below are some personality traits connected with the zodiac. Which animal is connected to your birth year?

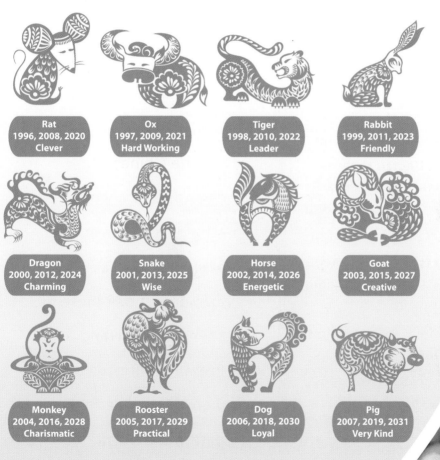

Rat
1996, 2008, 2020
Clever

Ox
1997, 2009, 2021
Hard Working

Tiger
1998, 2010, 2022
Leader

Rabbit
1999, 2011, 2023
Friendly

Dragon
2000, 2012, 2024
Charming

Snake
2001, 2013, 2025
Wise

Horse
2002, 2014, 2026
Energetic

Goat
2003, 2015, 2027
Creative

Monkey
2004, 2016, 2028
Charismatic

Rooster
2005, 2017, 2029
Practical

Dog
2006, 2018, 2030
Loyal

Pig
2007, 2019, 2031
Very Kind

Chinese New Year celebrations often feature the creatures and figures of Chinese mythology.

The first dozen to cross the finish line became the 12 zodiac symbols.

Food plays a big part in Chinese New Year celebrations. The meal always consists of eight courses. The number eight is considered lucky in Chinese culture. The final dish is often fish. Fish is considered lucky because the word for fish, *yu*, sounds like the word for wealth.

The color red is seen in many places during Chinese New Year celebrations. Mythology states that this color frightens off evil spirits. Black and white are considered mourning colors. They are often seen at funerals in China.

These traditions, along with other celebrations, help people keep Chinese mythology alive in the modern era. Some people still believe deeply in the Chinese gods and goddesses. They pass their stories on to their children so that they can keep the stories going when they grow up.

FURTHER EVIDENCE

Chapter Five discusses Chinese mythology in modern-day China. What is the main idea of this chapter? What key evidence supports this idea? Read the article at the website below. Find information from the site related to the main idea of this chapter. Does the information support an existing piece of evidence in the chapter, or does it add new evidence?

CHINESE NEW YEAR EXPLAINED
abdocorelibrary.com/chinese-mythology

FAST FACTS

Gods and Goddesses

- Huang Di is the Yellow Emperor. The most important of Taoism's five divine emperors, he is also known as the Thunder God.

- Changxi is the mother of the ten moons.

- Chiyou is the god of war.

- Xihe is the mother of the ten suns.

- Xiwangmu is the Chinese goddess of immortality.

- Shennong is the god of Chinese medicine.

Creatures

- Kui is a water monster that looks like a one-legged ox. Huang Di made a drum from this creature's hide.

- Yinglong is a winged dragon who brings rain. He helped Huang Di defeat his enemy Chiyou.

- Xiangliu is a giant black snake with nine human heads that poisoned the earth wherever he traveled.

Stories

- Some myths say the universe was created from the dead body of Pangu, the first divine human.

- The goddess Nüwa is said to have created human beings by molding them from mud.

- Gun and Yu are a father and son who spent their lives trying to control a flood. Yu succeeded and is a great hero in Chinese mythology.

STOP AND
THINK

Say What?

Reading a book about Chinese mythology can mean learning a lot of new vocabulary. Find five words in this book that you had not seen before. Use a dictionary to find out what they mean. Then write the meanings in your own words, and use each word in a new sentence.

You Are There

This book talks about several well-known Chinese myths. Imagine that you witnessed the events in one of these stories yourself. Write a letter home telling your family and friends about your experience. Be sure to add plenty of details.

Dig Deeper

After reading this book, what questions do you still have about a specific Chinese god or goddess? With an adult's help, find a few reliable sources that will help you answer these questions. Write a paragraph about what you learned.

Why Do I Care?

Even if you are not familiar with many Chinese myths, you have probably seen things inspired by these myths in your everyday life. Think about things from Chapter Five that you have seen or heard of before. Why do you think it is useful to learn about the history and stories behind these things?

GLOSSARY

Buddhism
a religion based on the teachings of a figure named the Buddha

Confucianism
traditions connected to the teachings of the Chinese scholar Confucius

cowherd
a person who tends cattle

deity
a god or goddess

divine
having the qualities of a god

drought
a long period with no rain

incense
a material that is burned to produce a fragrant odor

magpie
a bird with a long tail and black and white feathers

mortal
a living being that is able to die

ritual
a custom done in a specific way

Taoism
a Chinese religion and philosophy related to living in harmony with the universe

ONLINE RESOURCES

To learn more about Chinese gods, heroes, and mythology, visit our free resource websites below.

Core Library
CONNECTION
FREE! COMMON CORE MULTIMEDIA RESOURCES

Visit **abdocorelibrary.com** for free Common Core resources for teachers and students, including vetted activities, multimedia, and booklinks, for deeper subject comprehension.

Booklinks
NONFICTION NETWORK
FREE! ONLINE NONFICTION RESOURCES

Visit **abdobooklinks.com** for free additional online weblinks for further learning. These links are routinely monitored and updated to provide the most current information available.

LEARN MORE

LaPierre, Yvette. *Engineering the Great Wall of China.* Minneapolis, MN: Abdo, 2018.

Yasuda, Anita. *The Jade Emperor: A Chinese Zodiac Myth.* Minneapolis, MN: Abdo, 2014.

INDEX

About the Author

Tammy Gagne has written dozens of books for both adults and children. Her recent titles include *Women in Engineering* and *Exploring the Southwest*. She lives in northern New England with her husband, son, and pets.